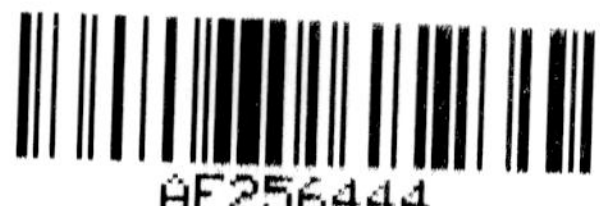

Geometric Patterns Coloring Book

Volume 2

Kristin Preachers

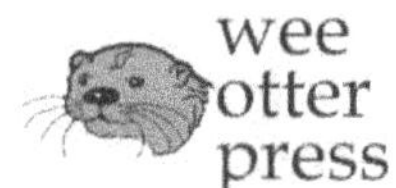

Wee Otter Press
Chattanooga, TN
www.weeotterpress.com

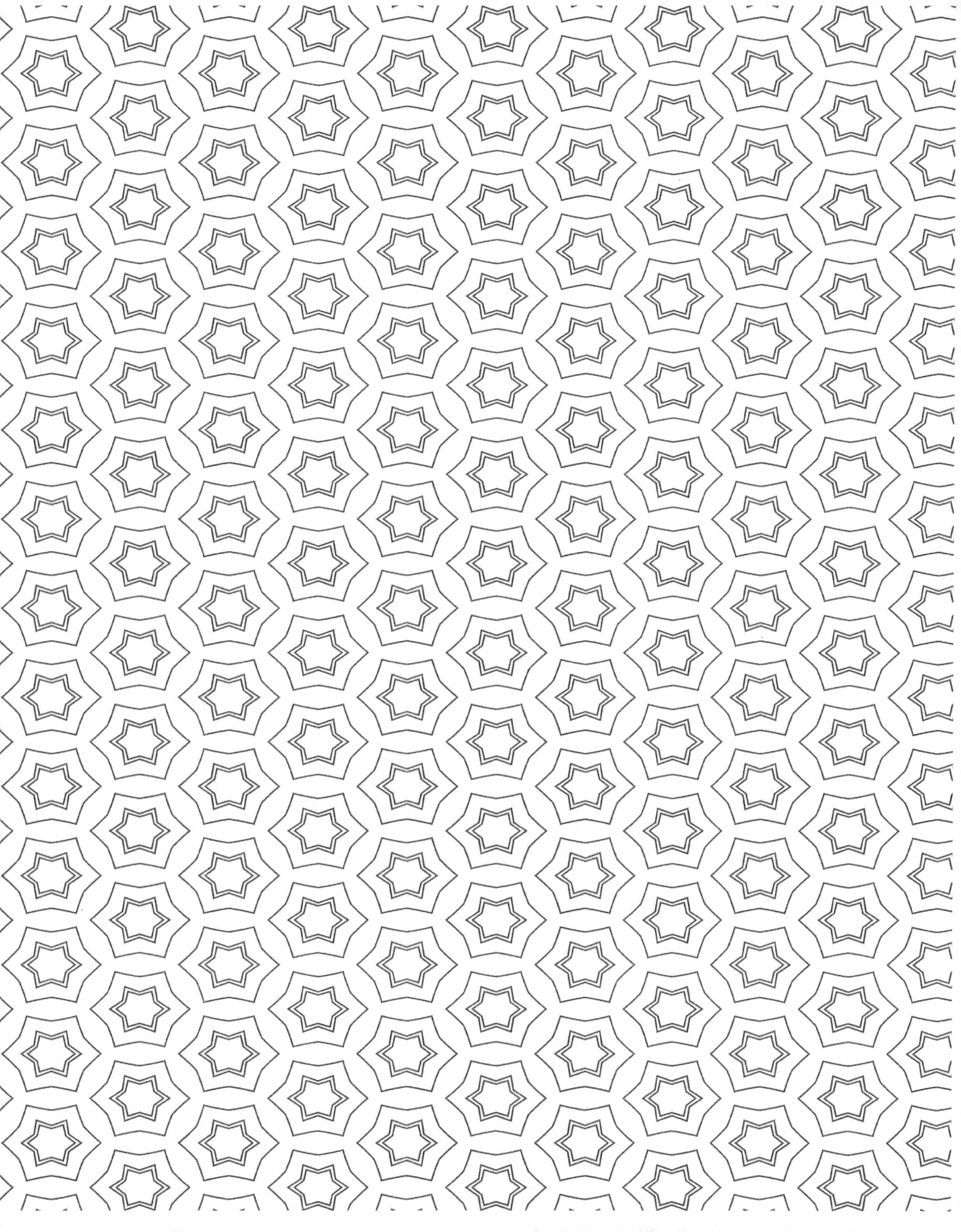

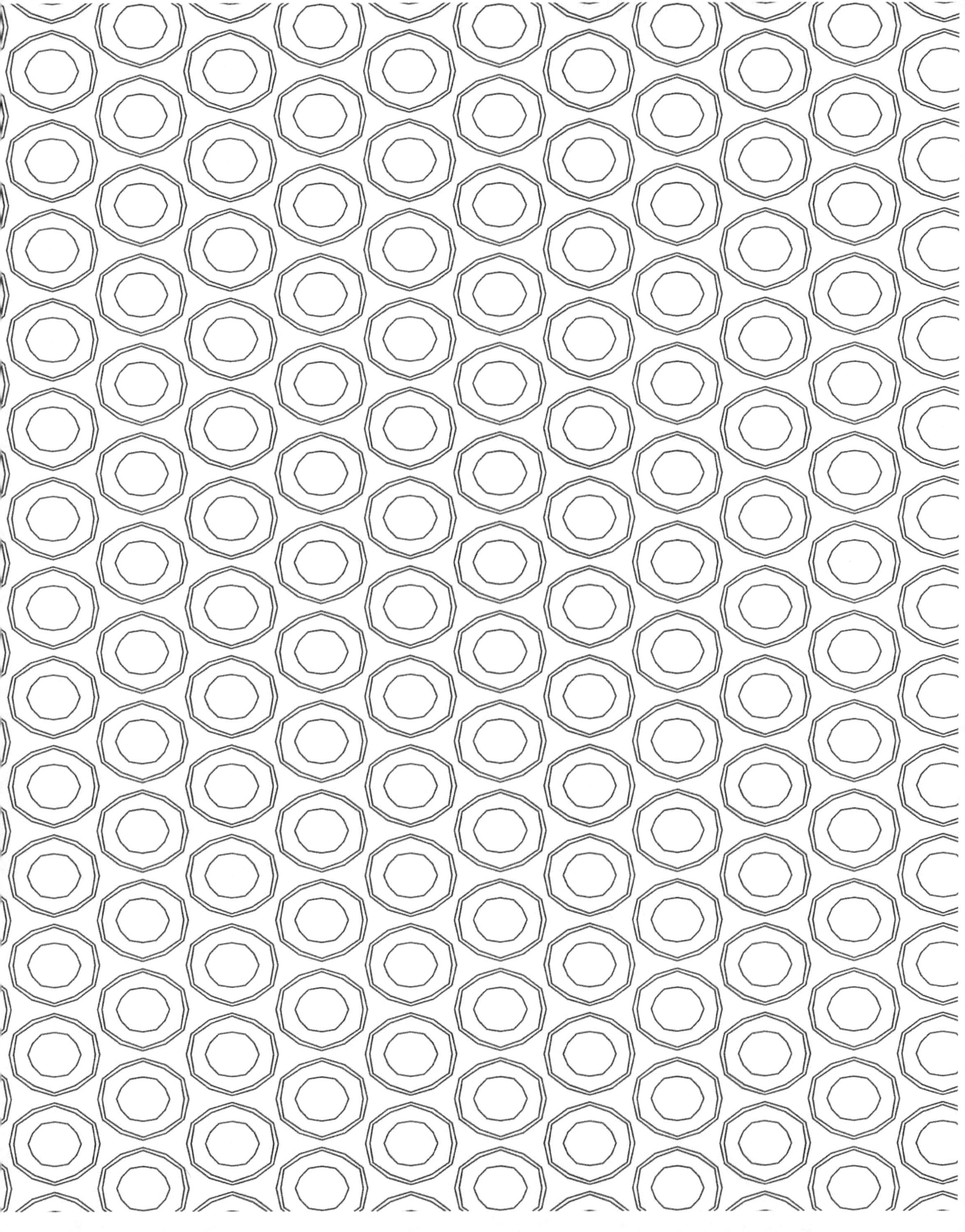

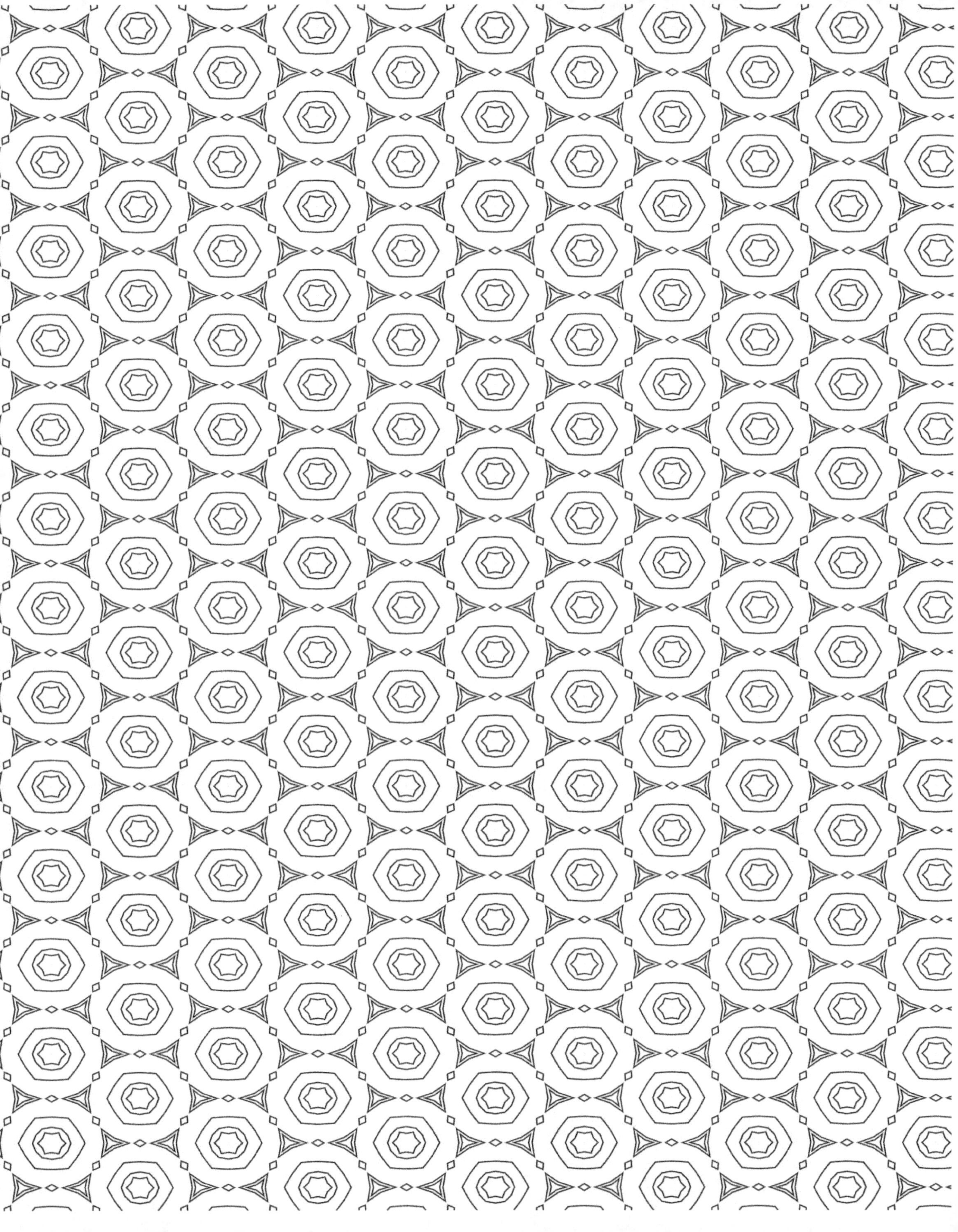

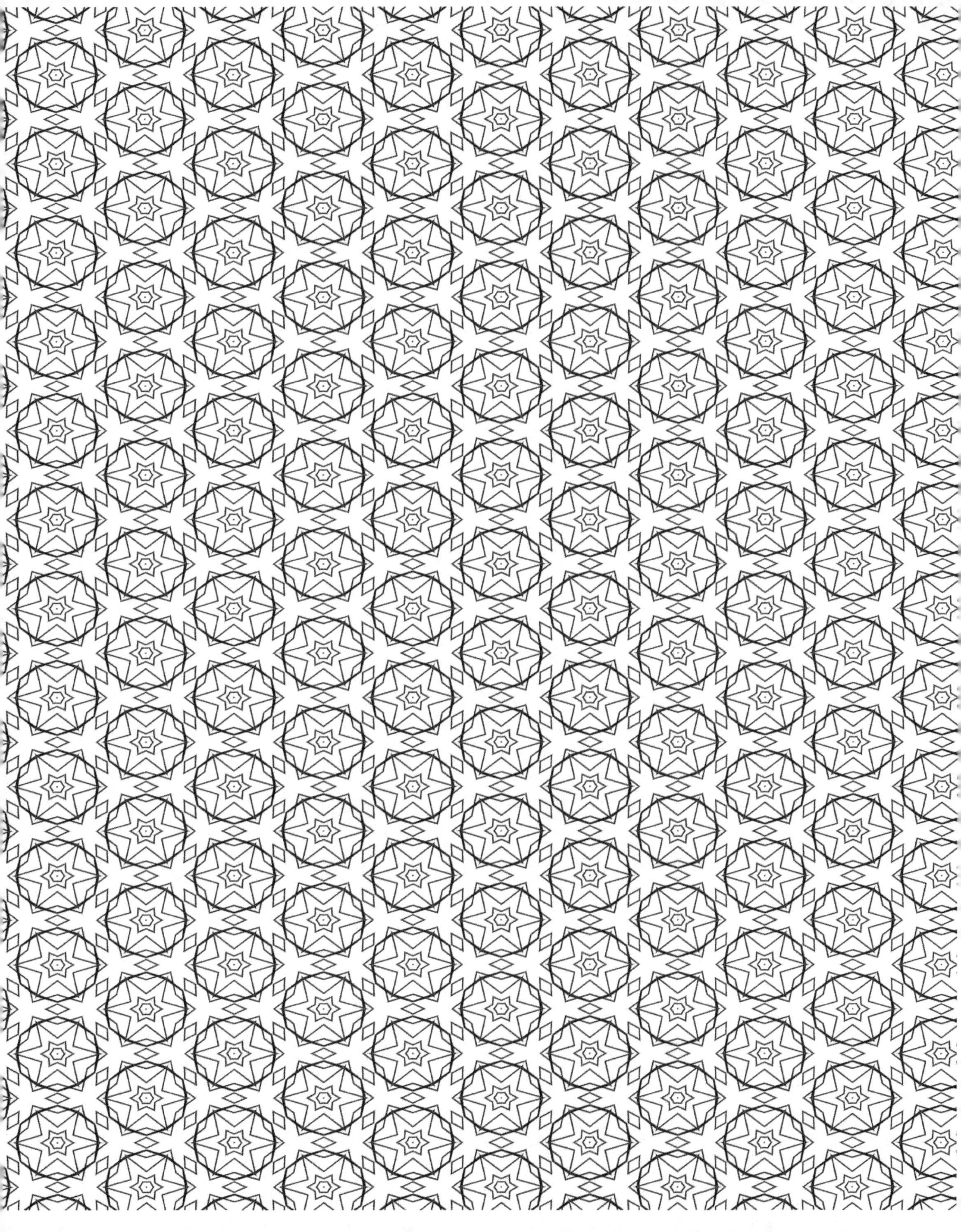

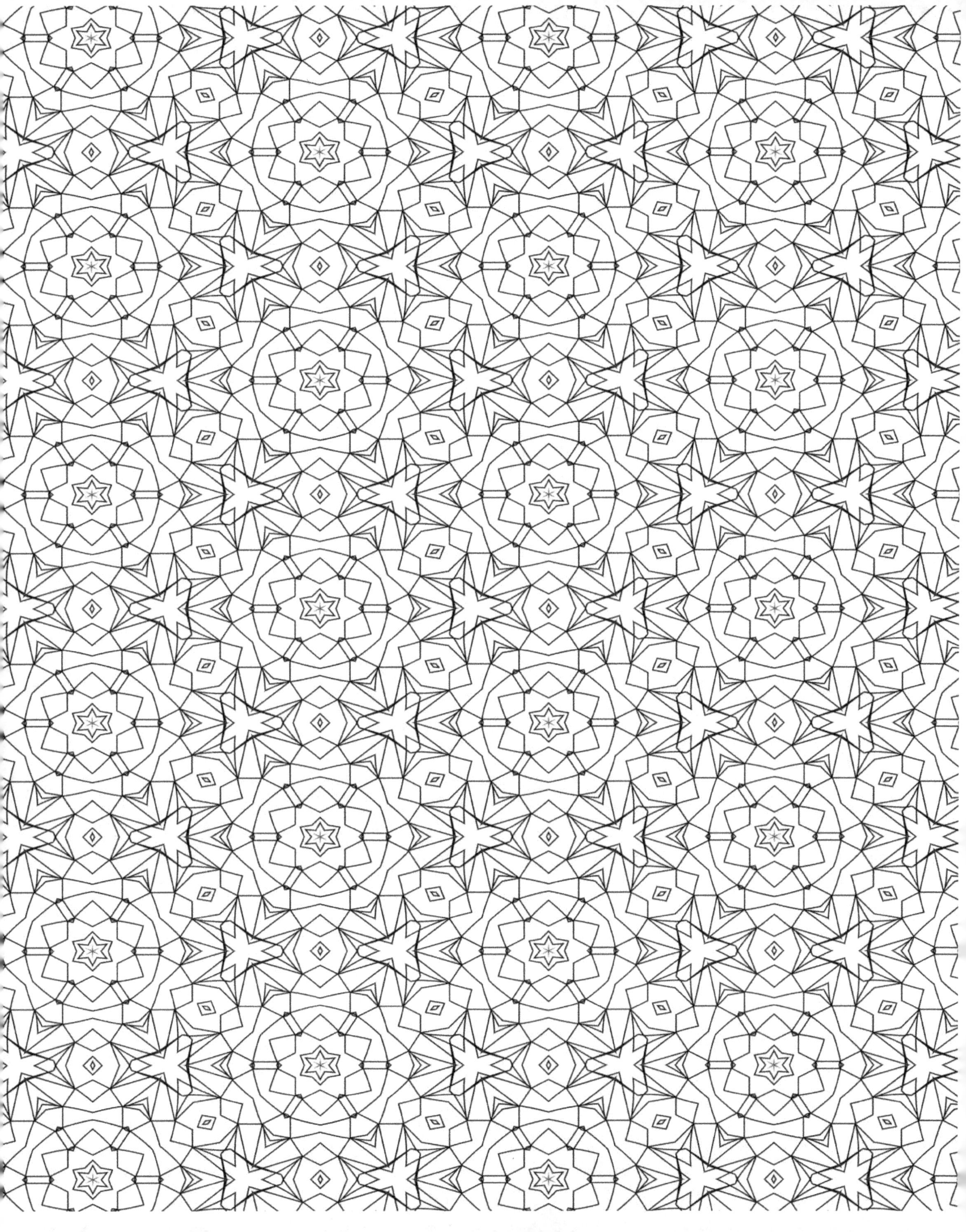

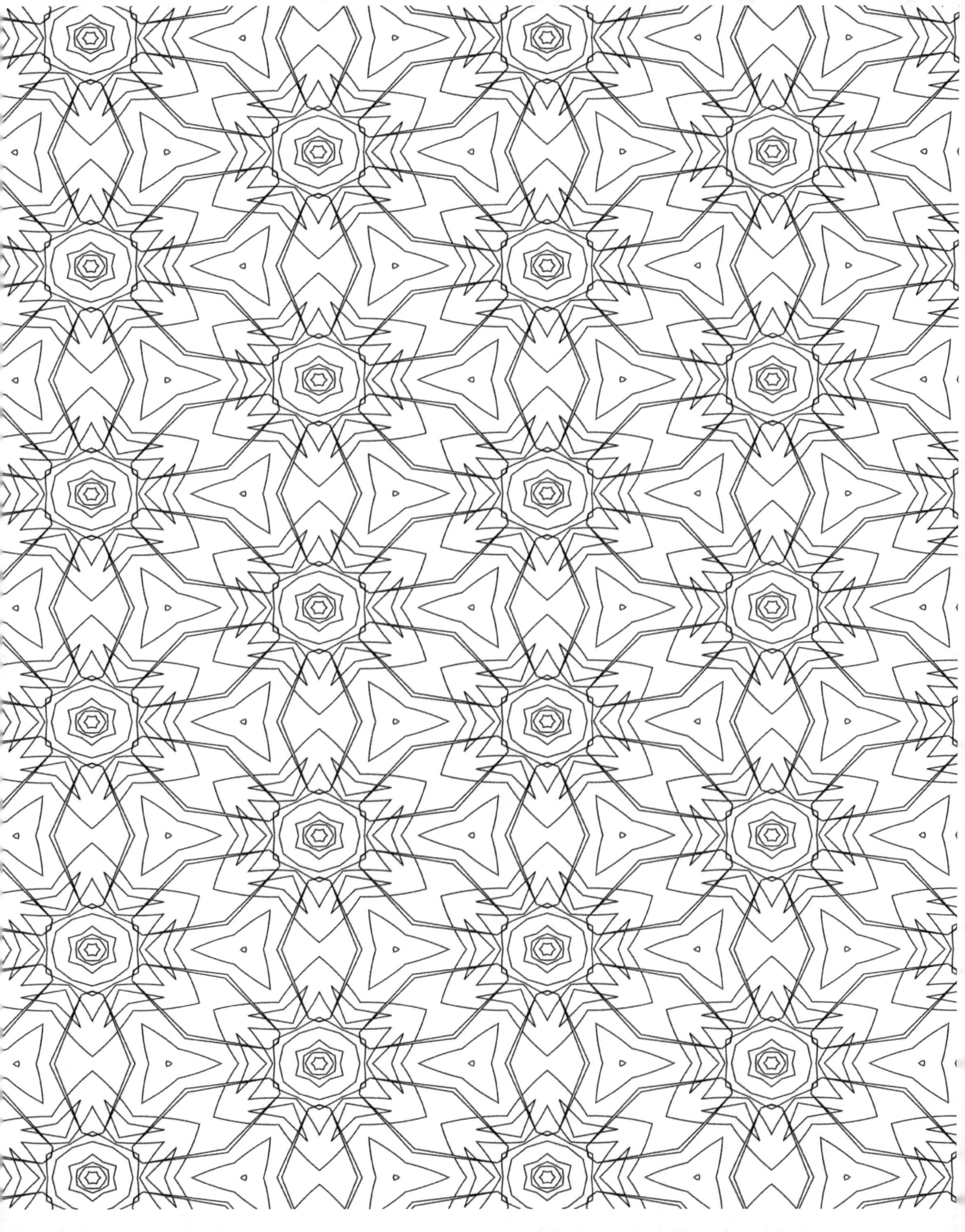

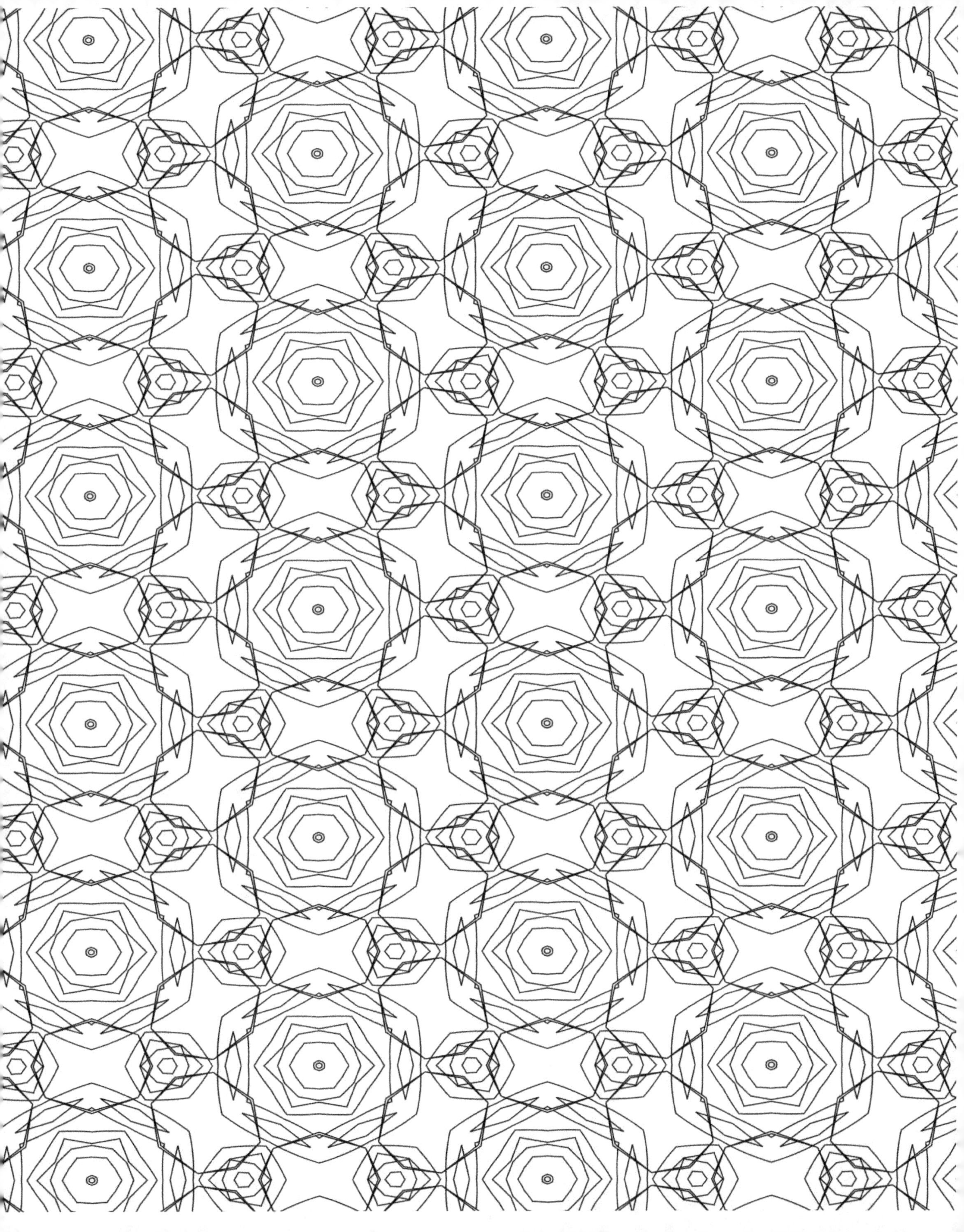

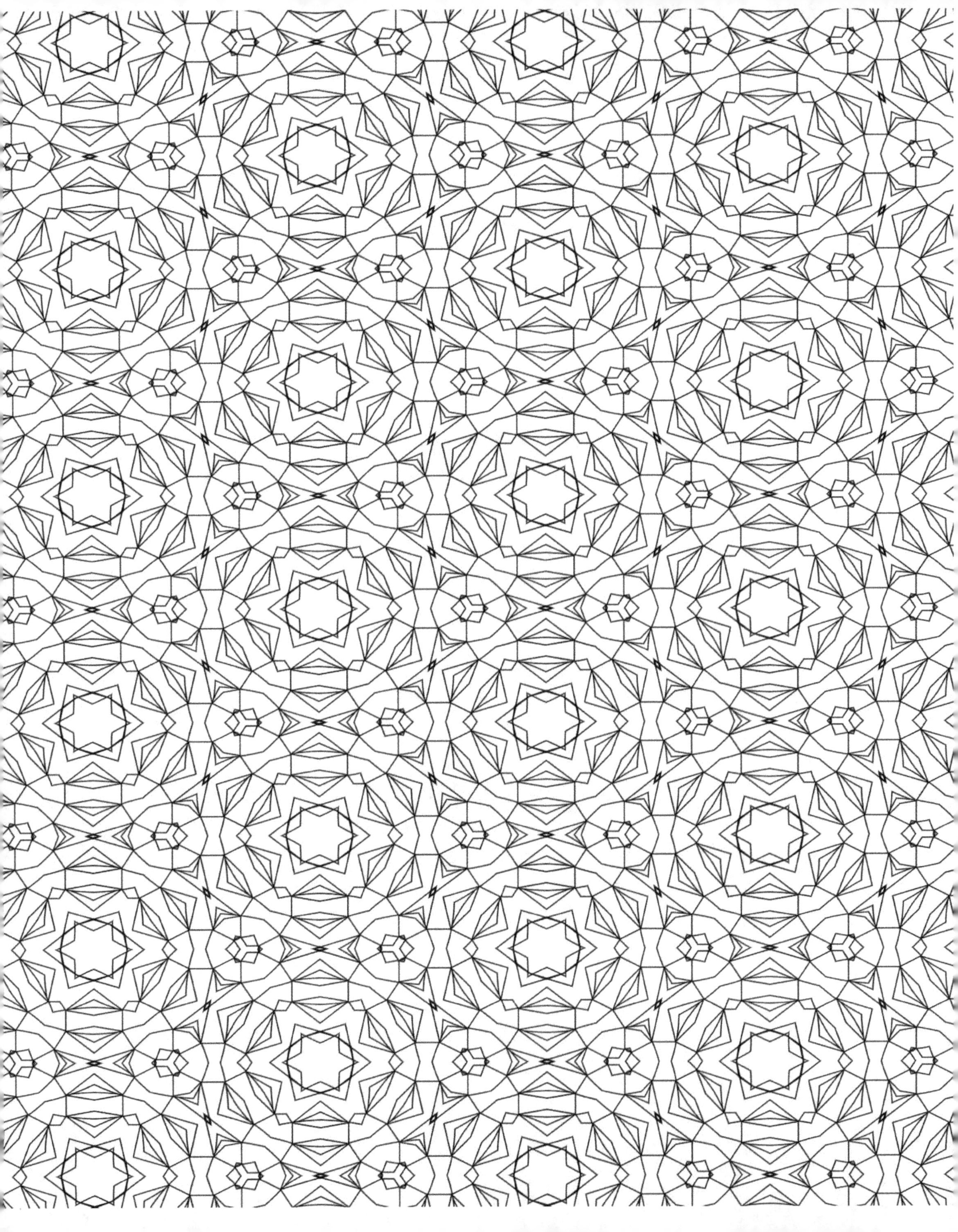

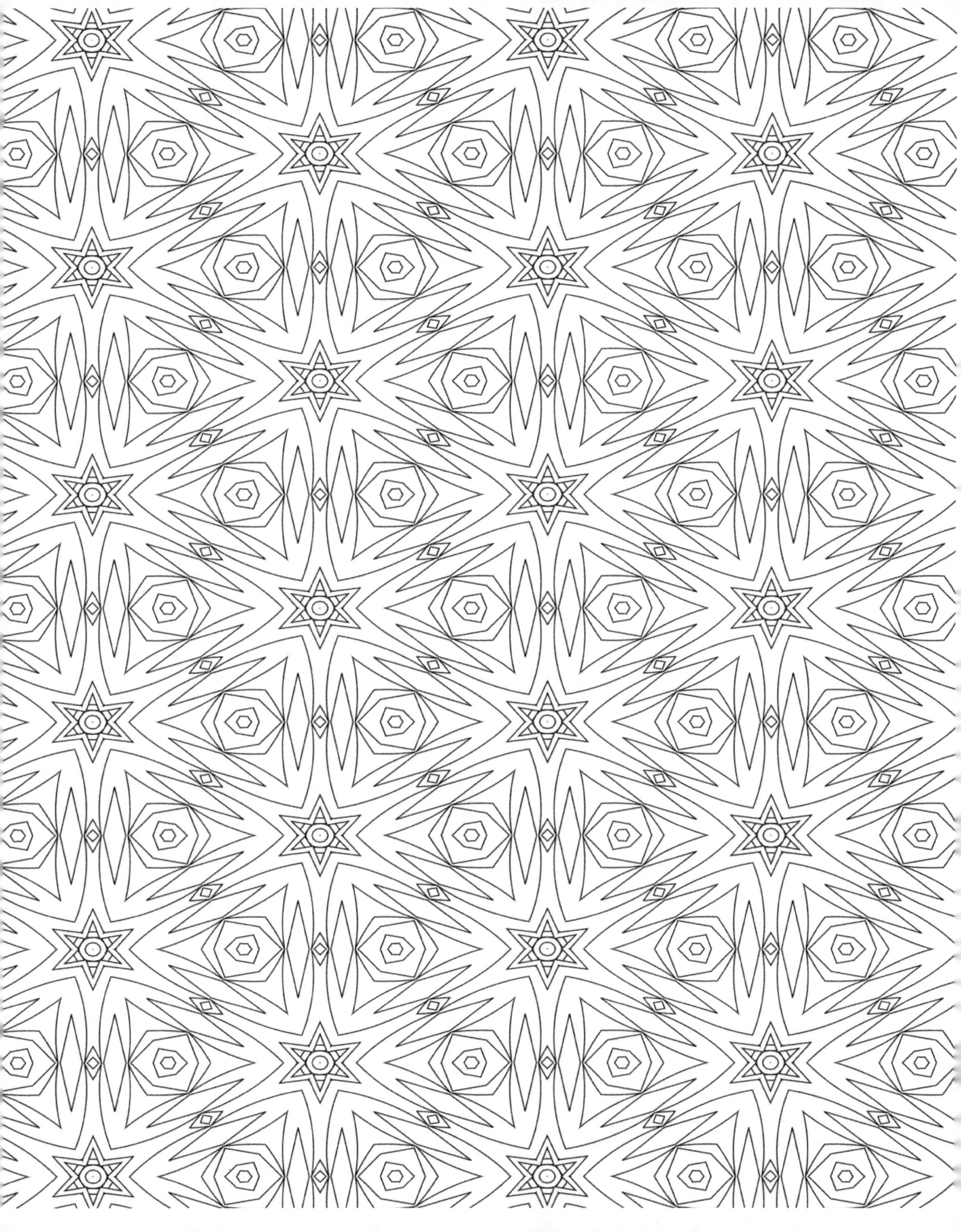

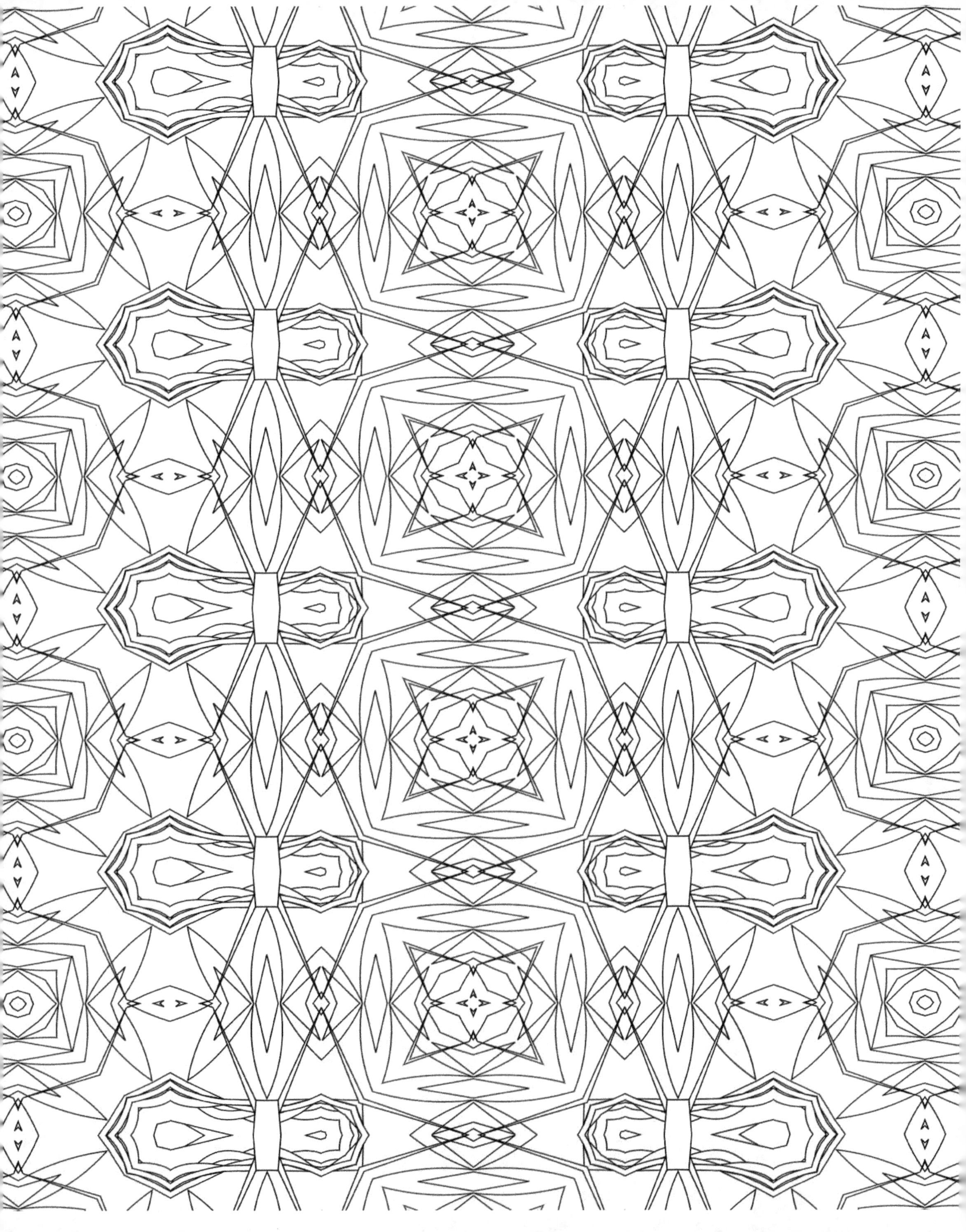

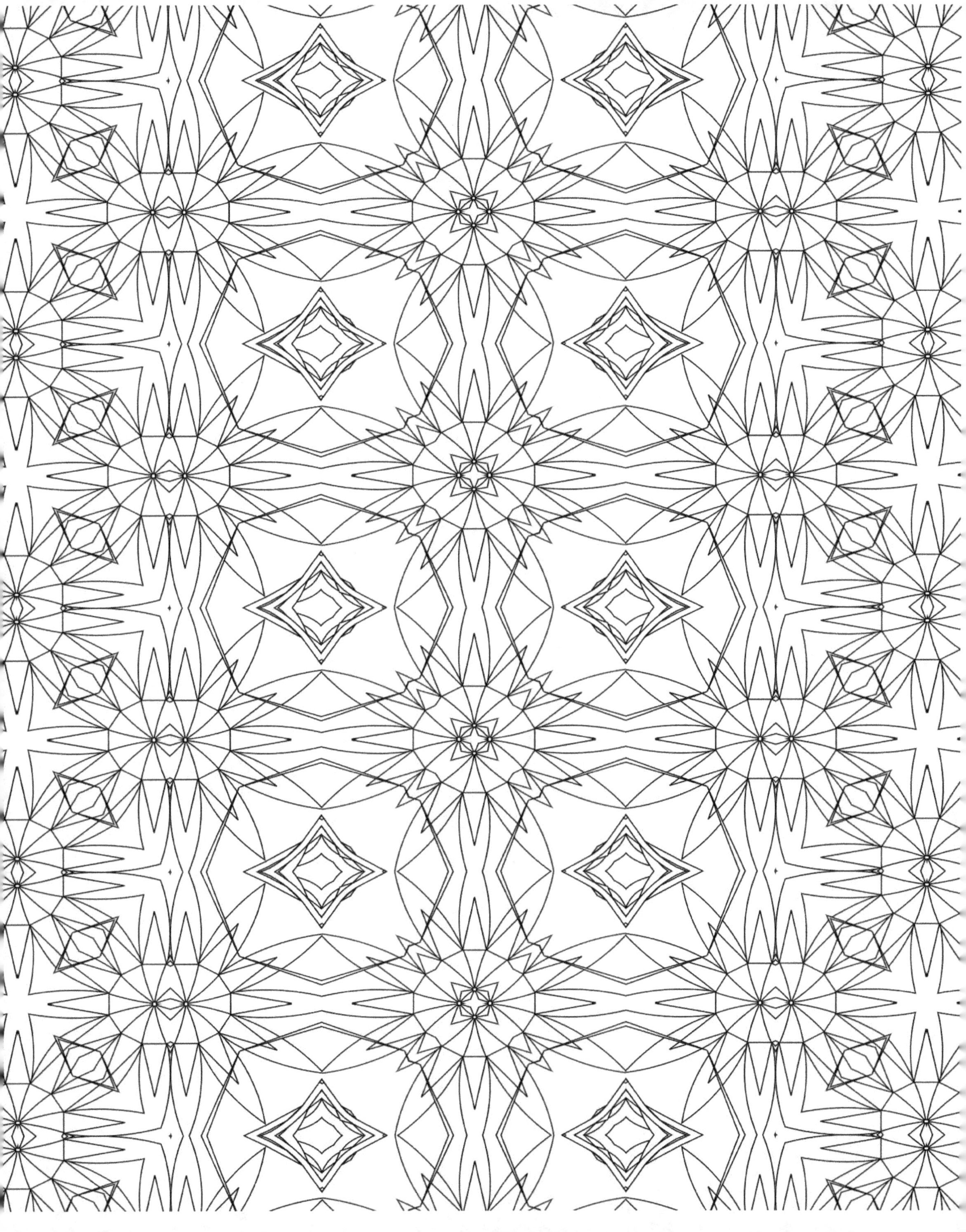

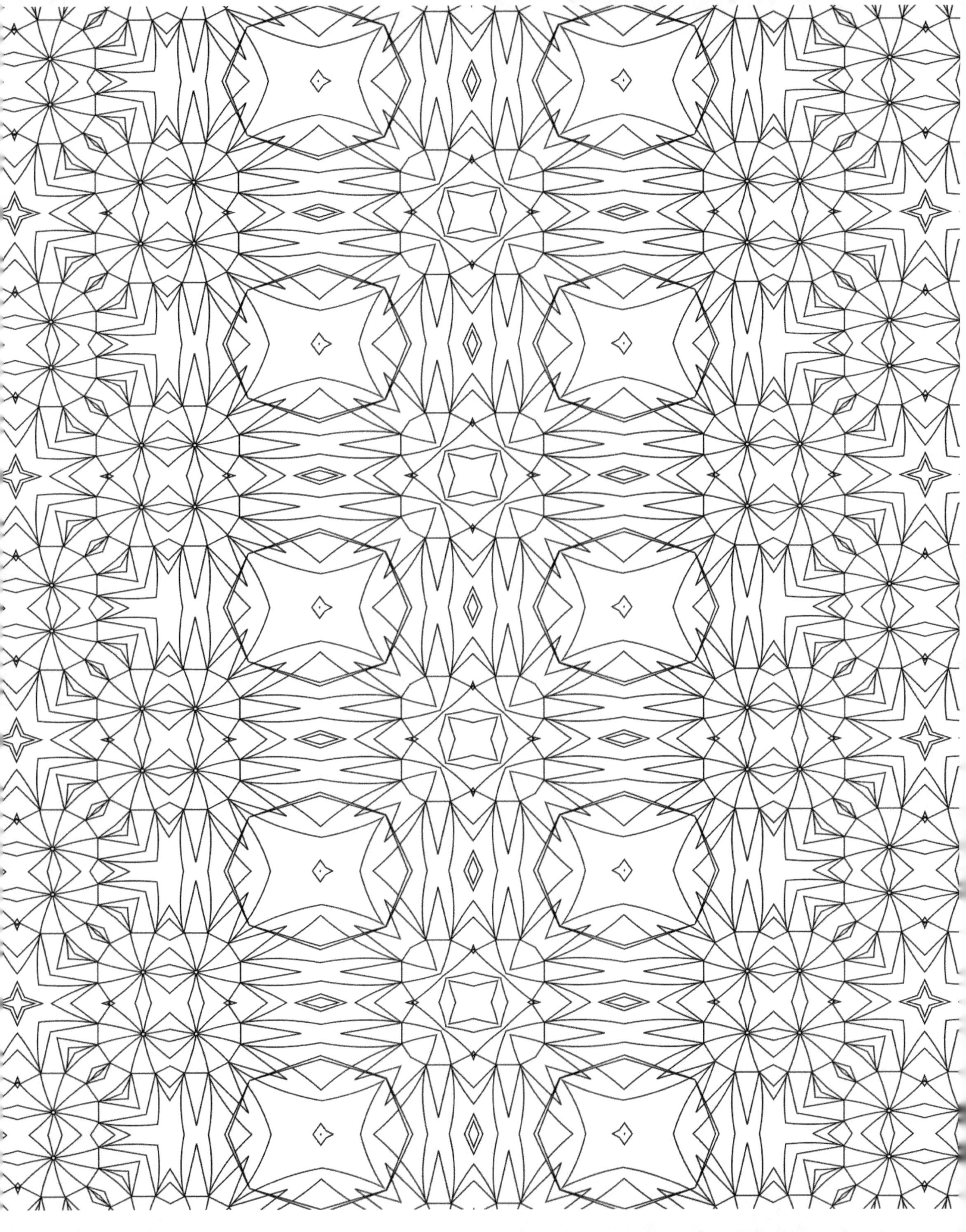

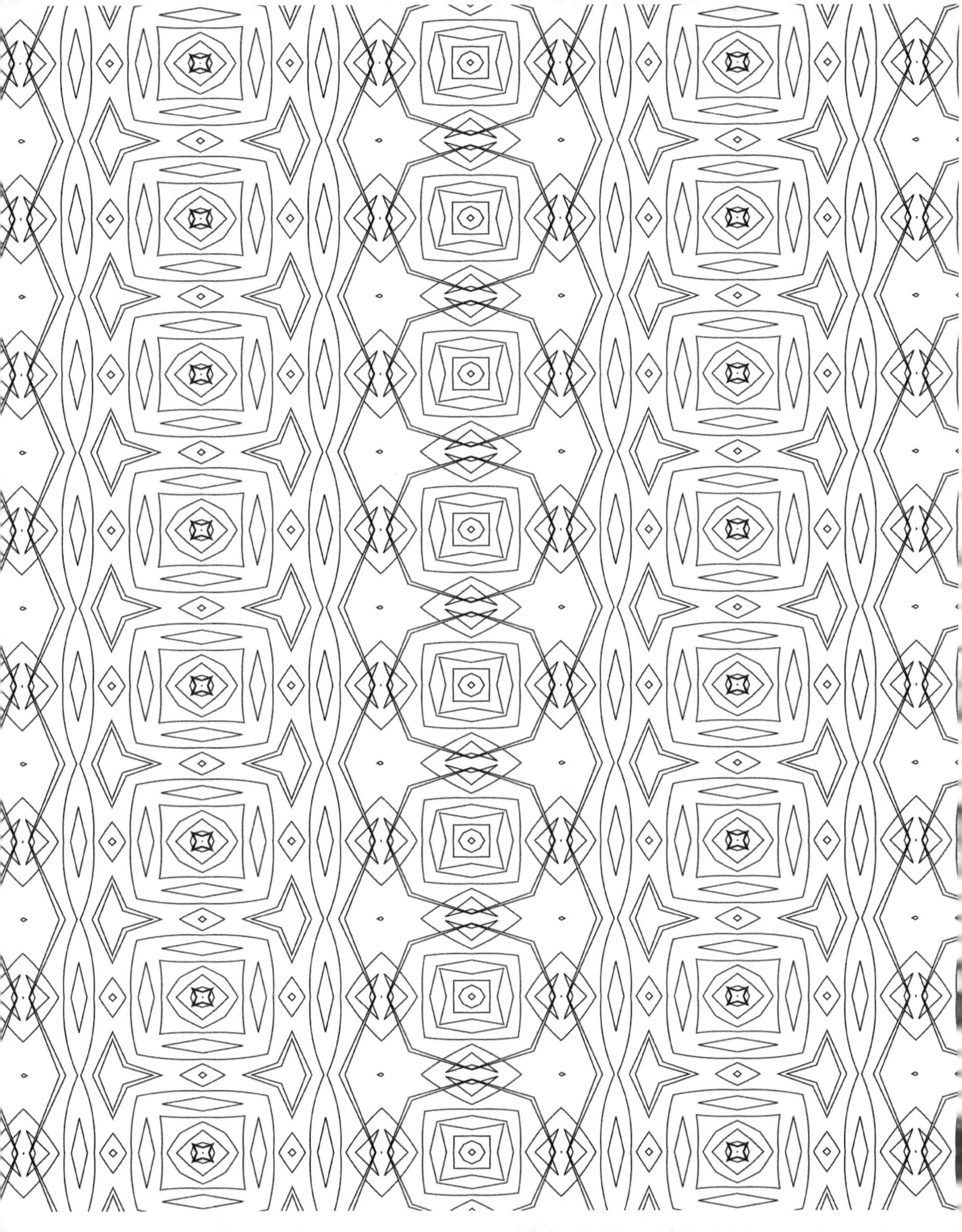

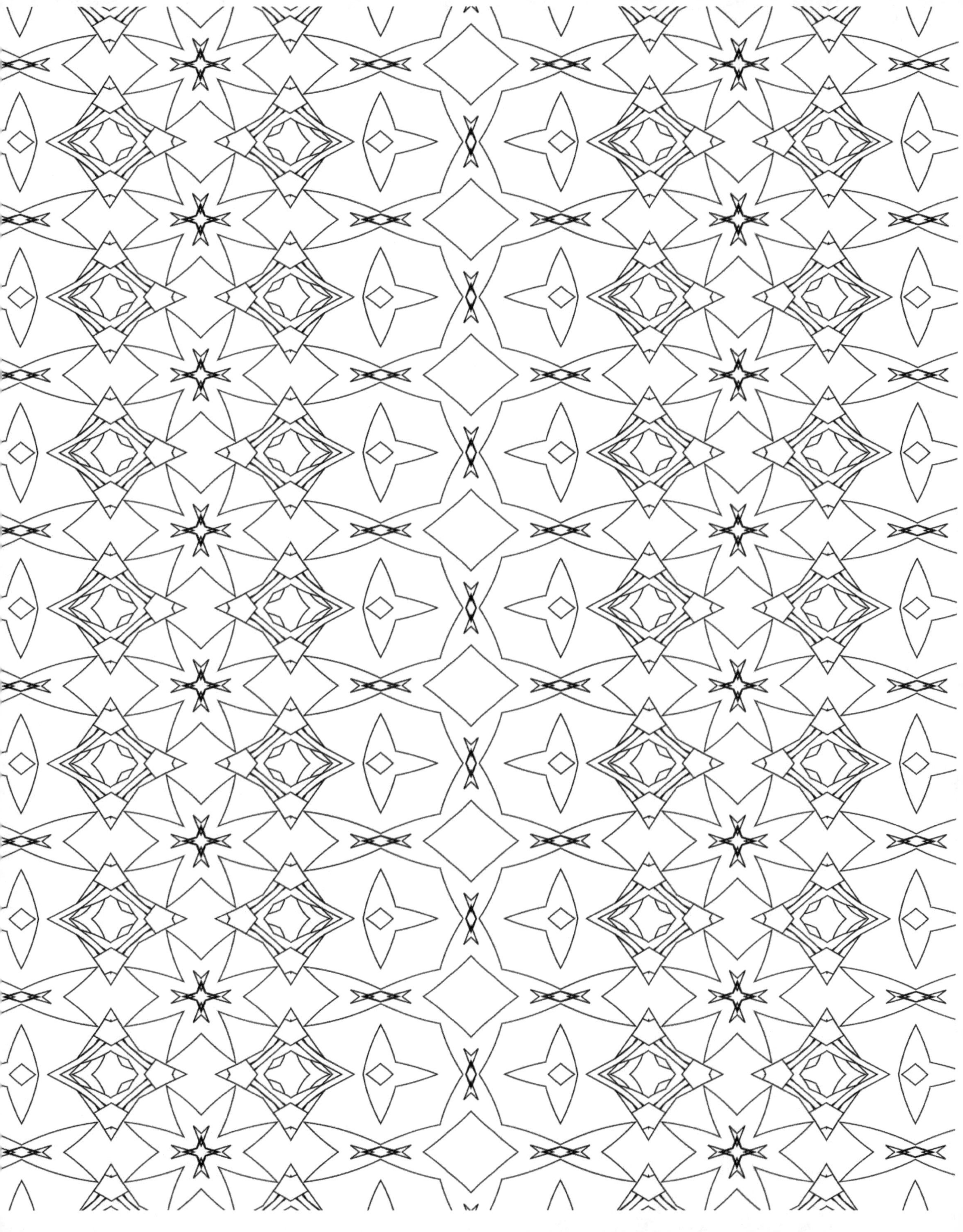

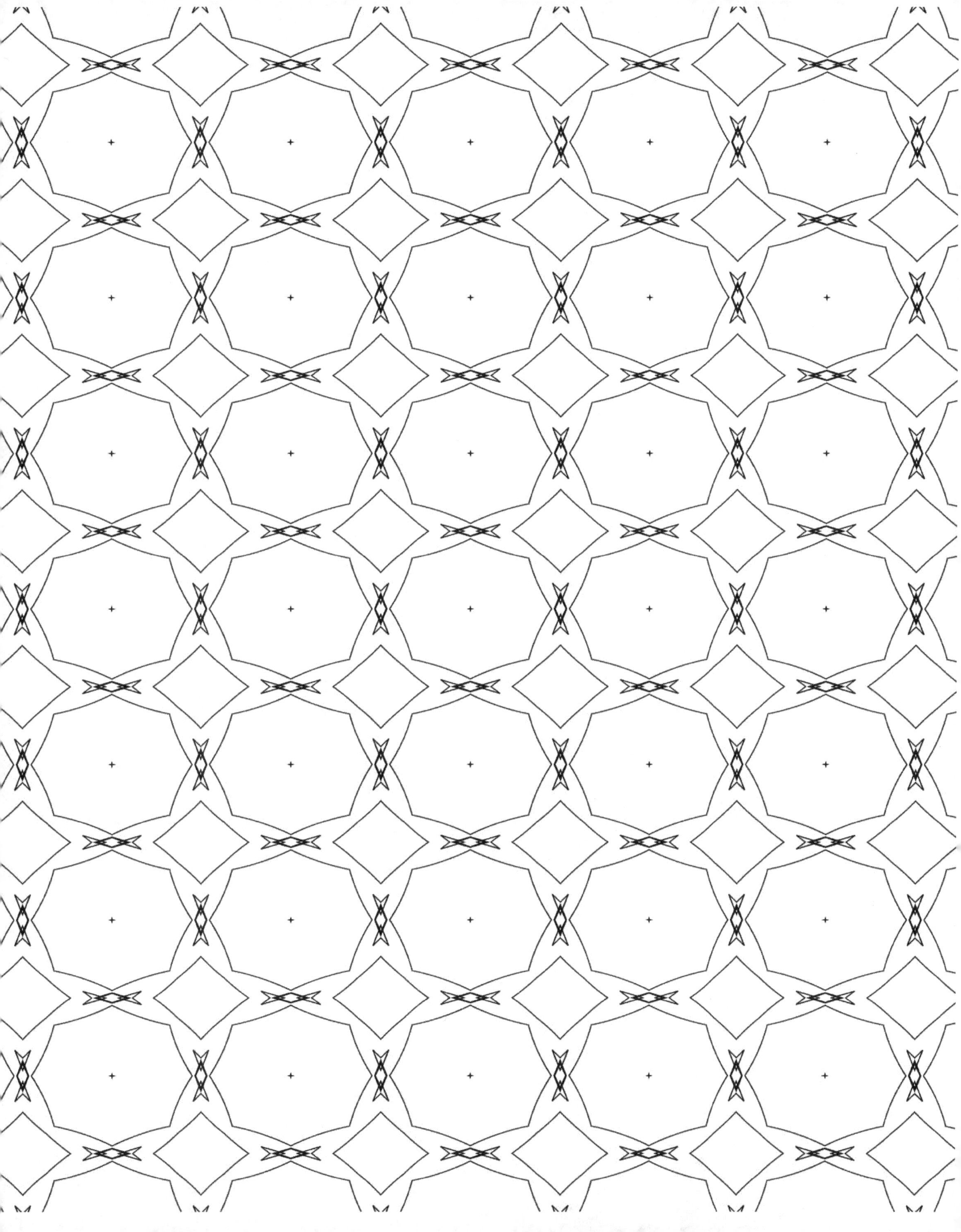

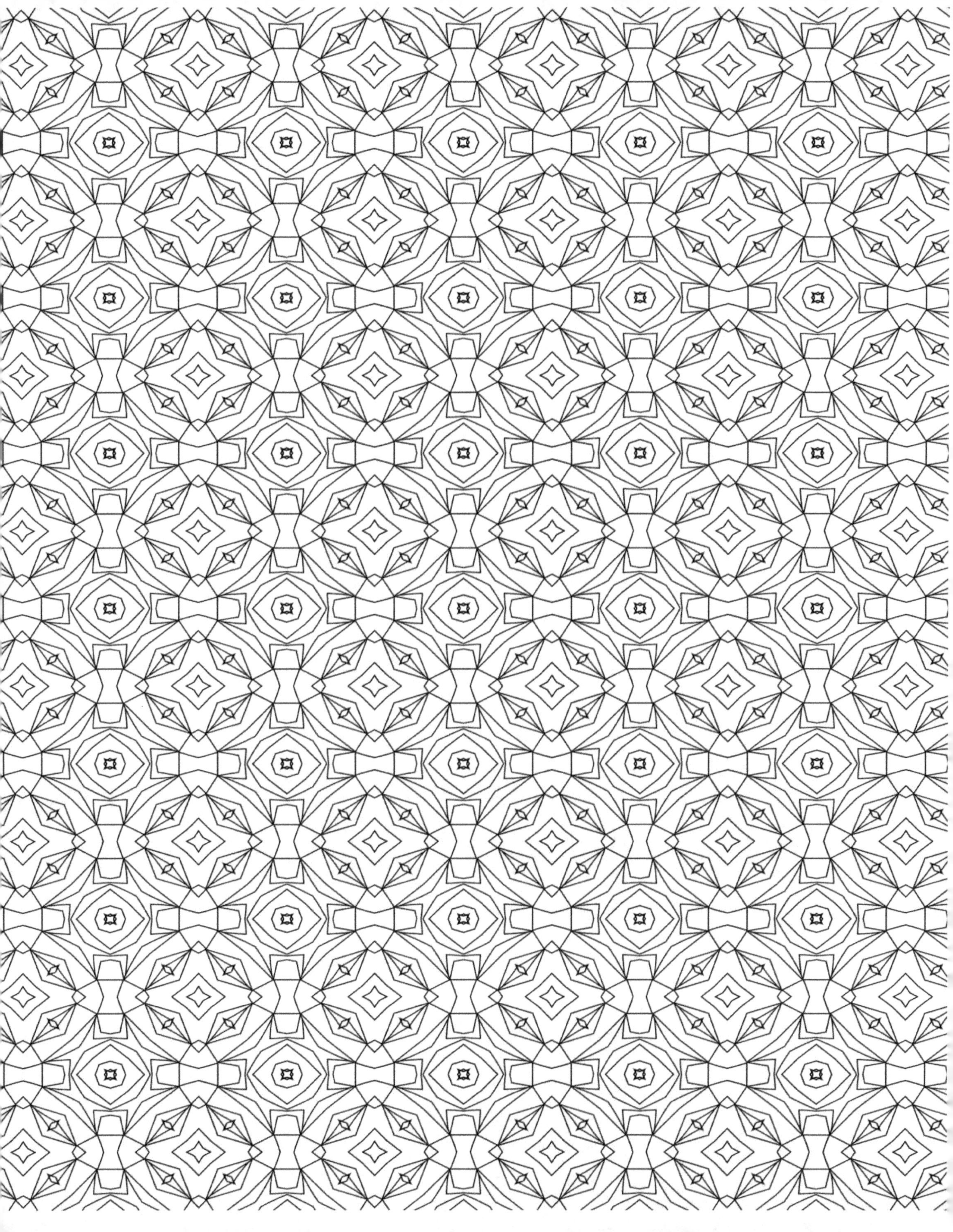

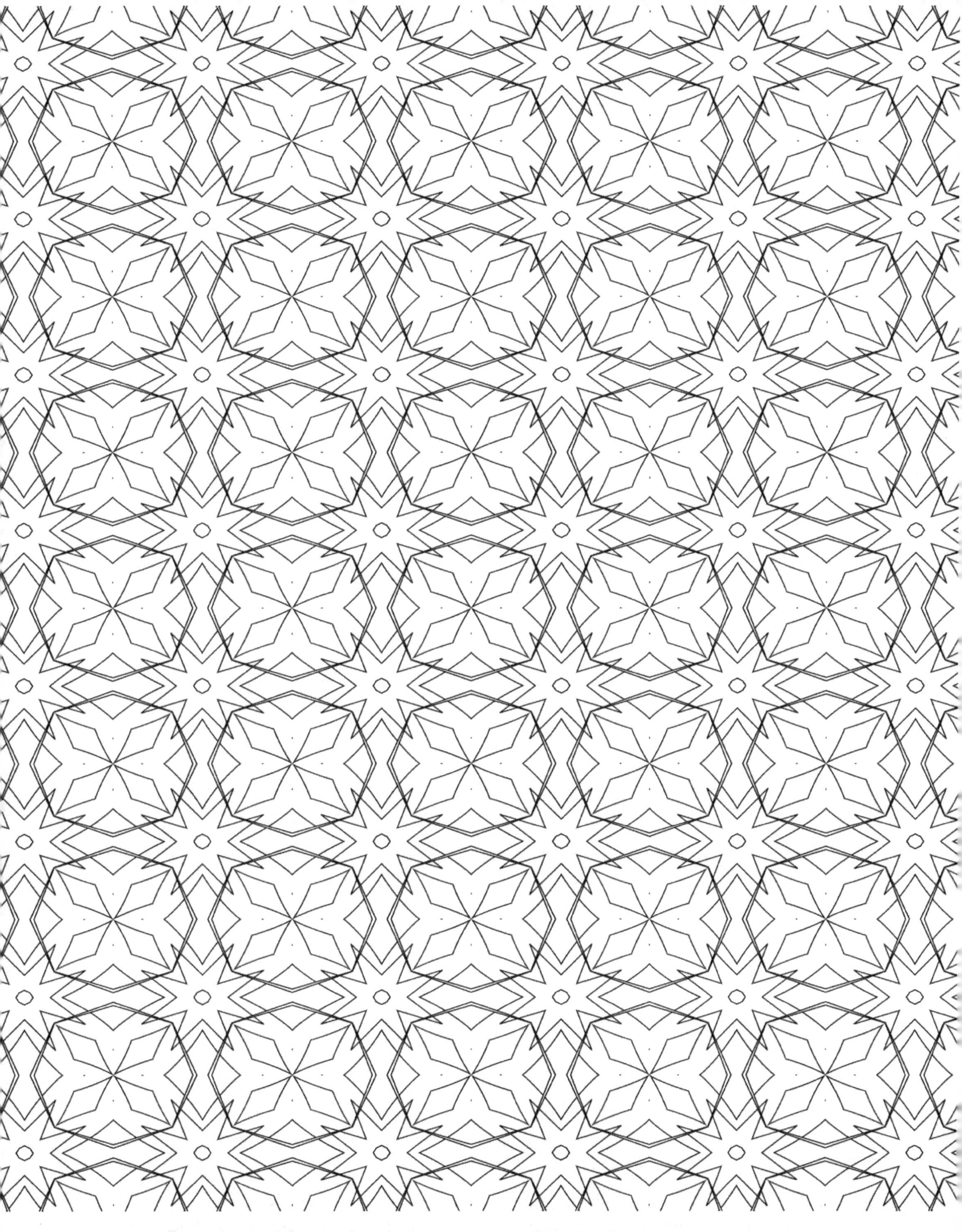

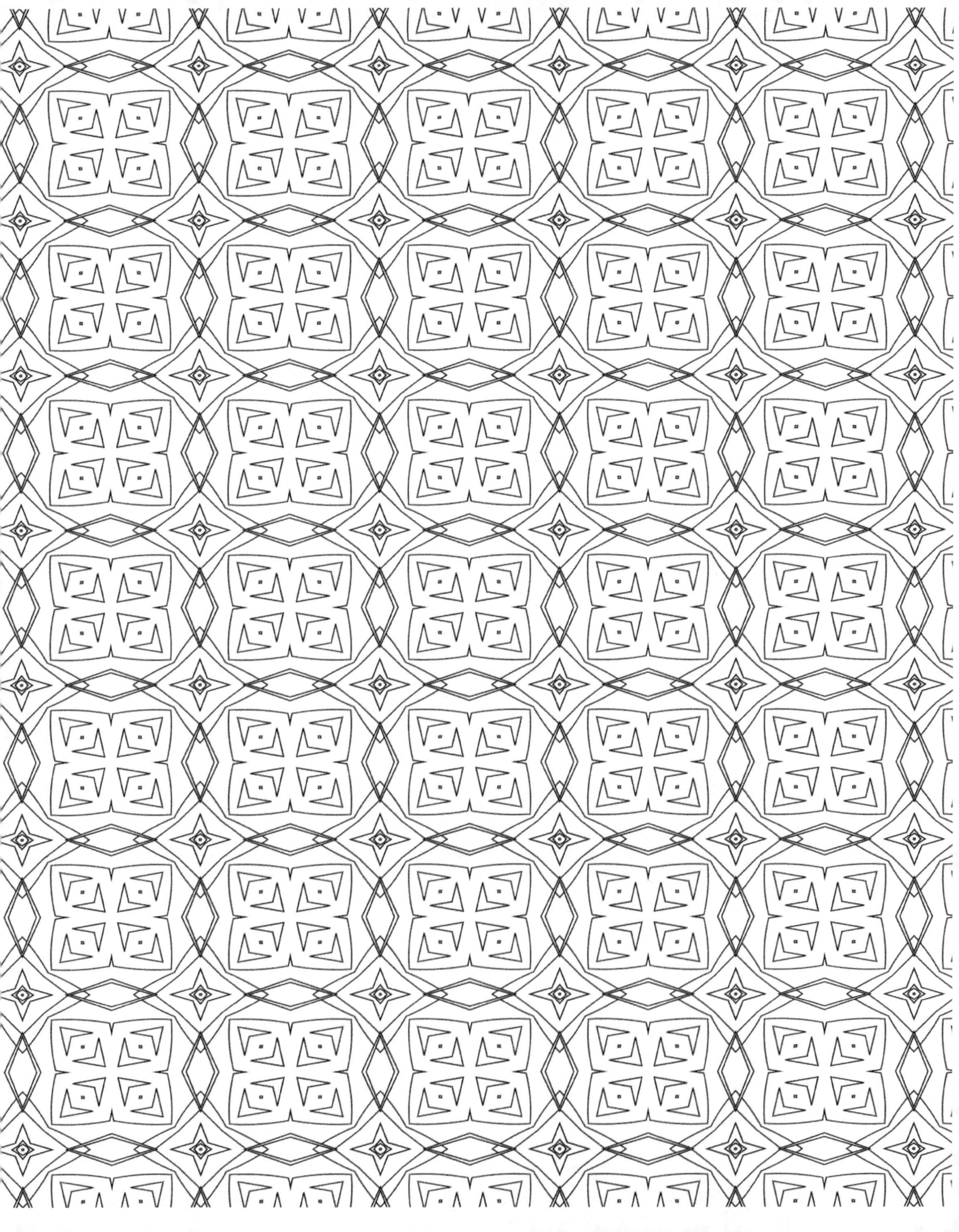

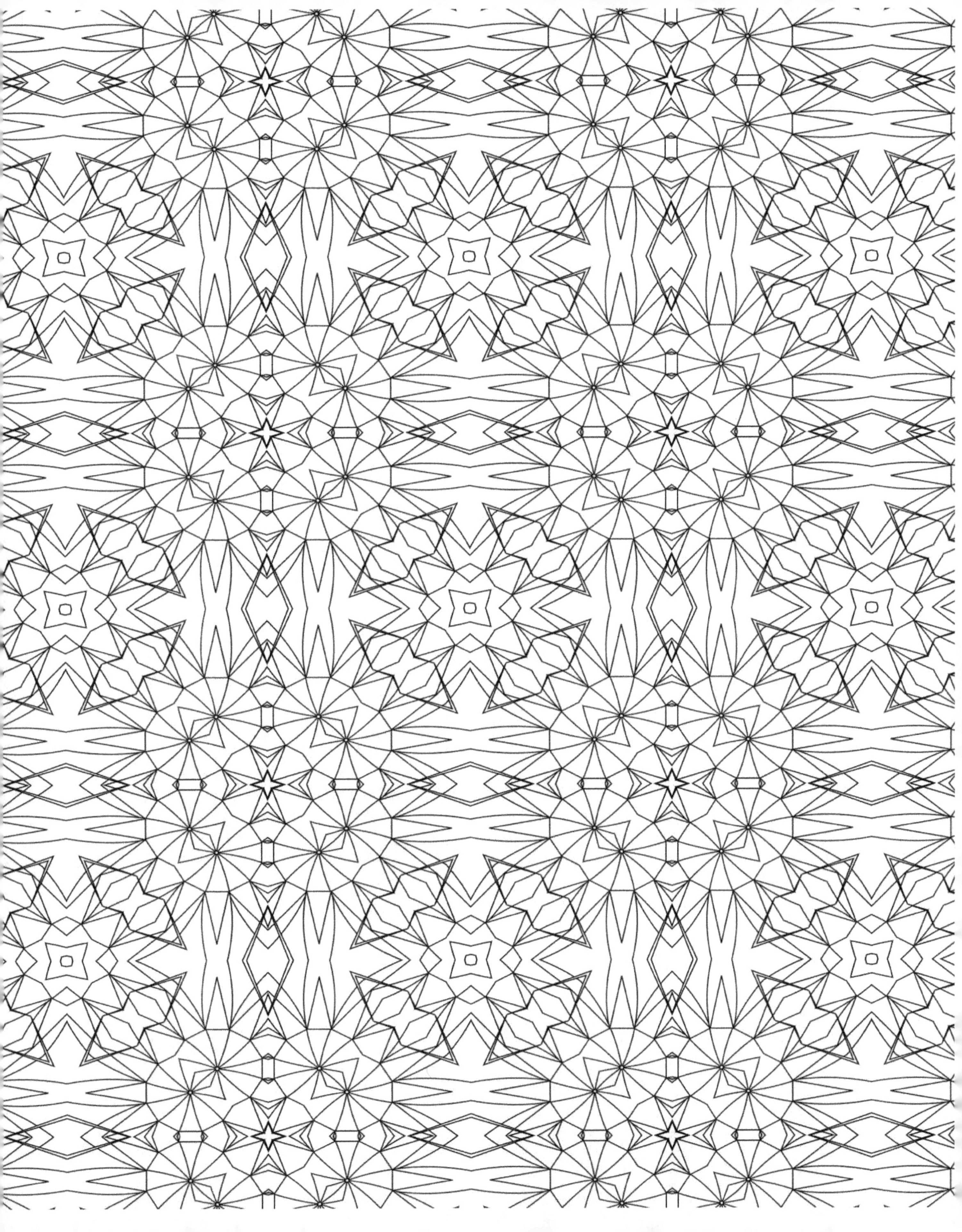

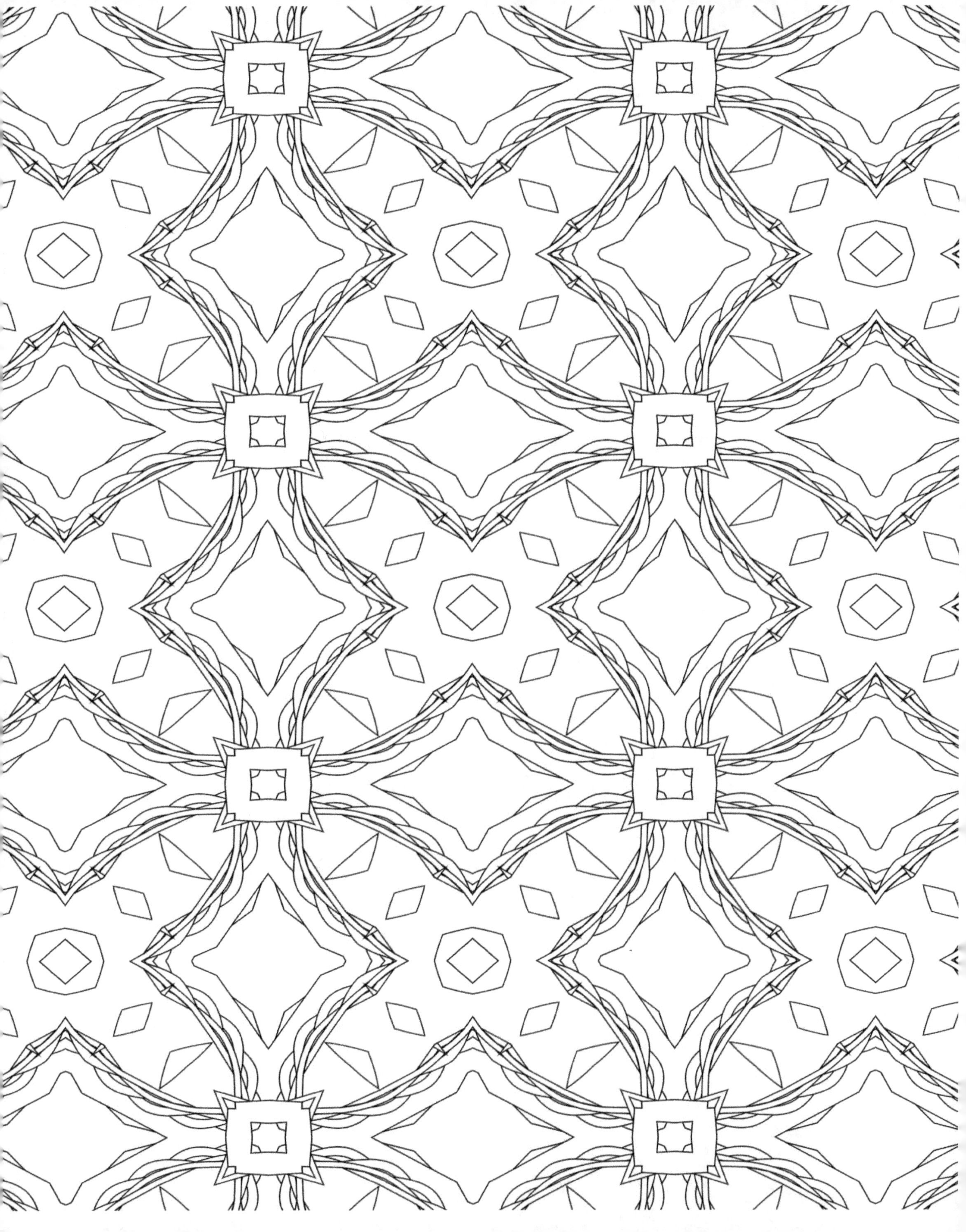

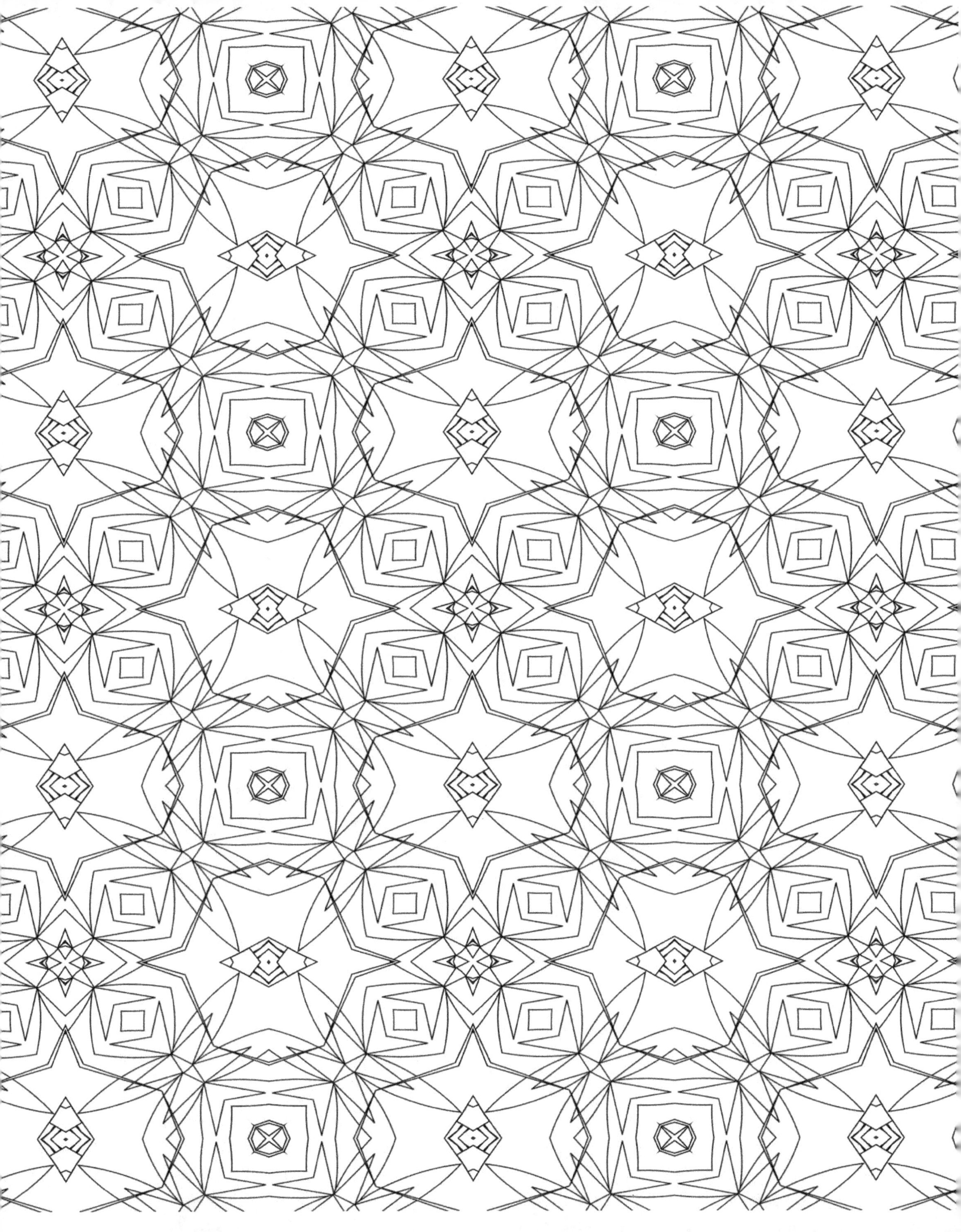

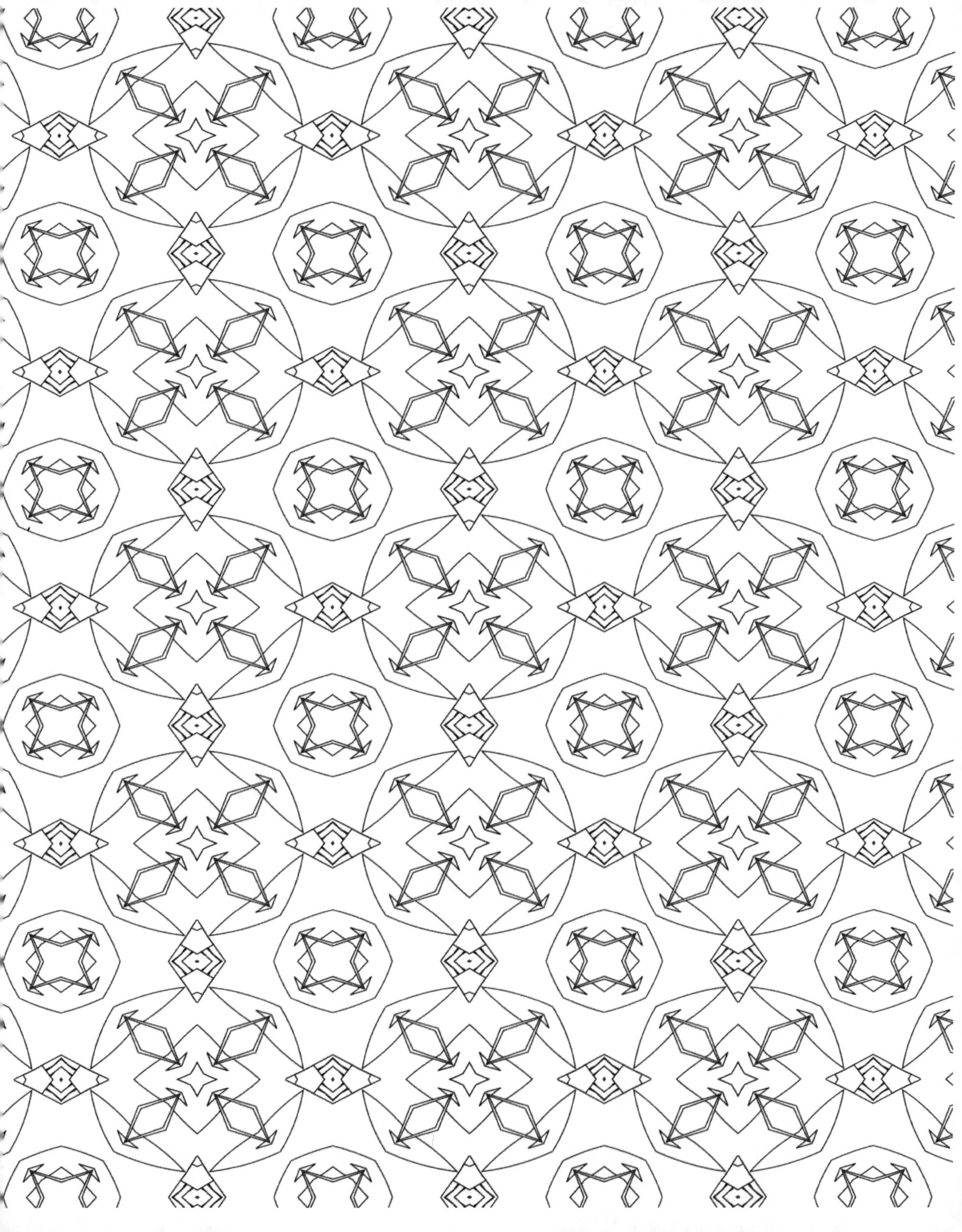

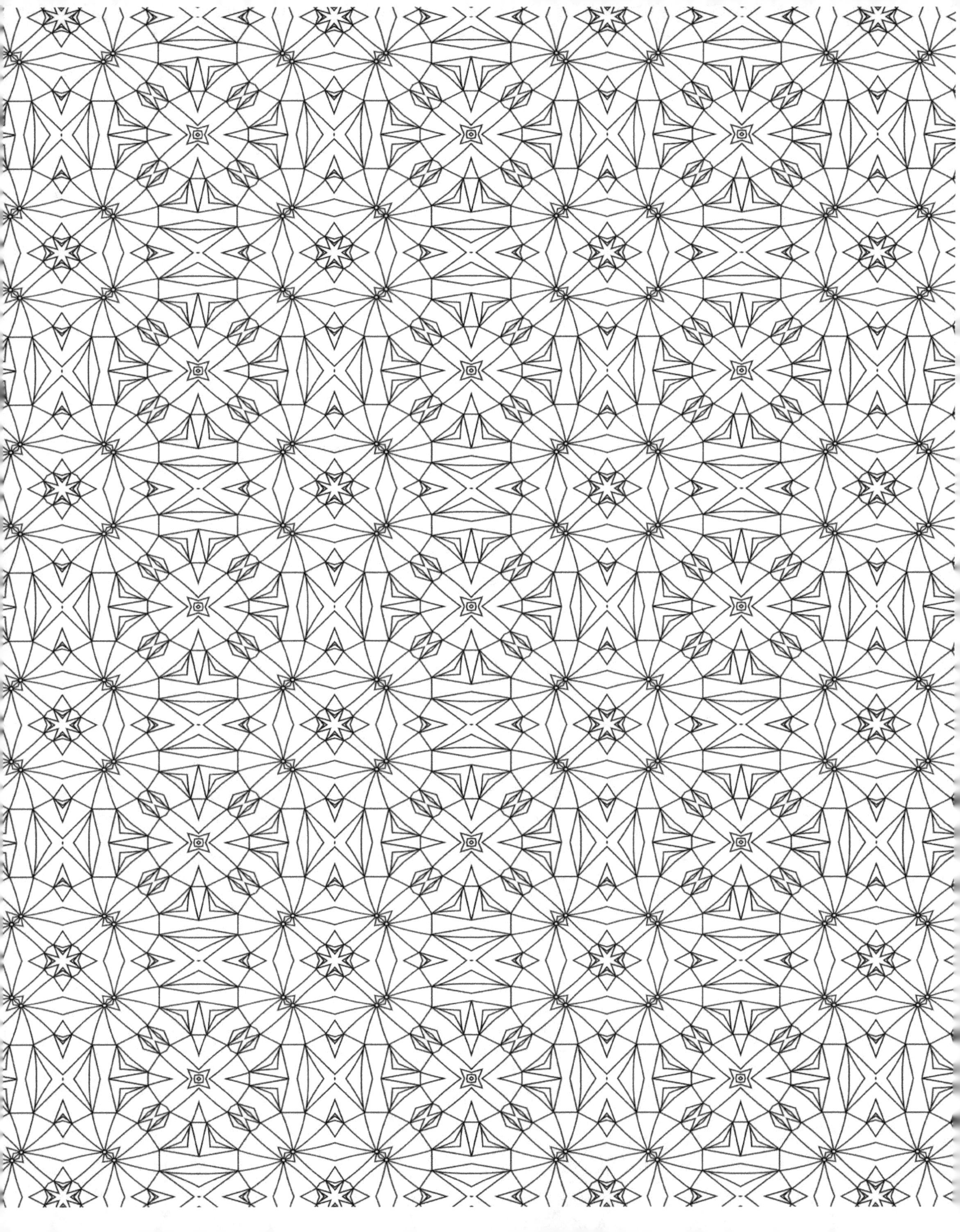

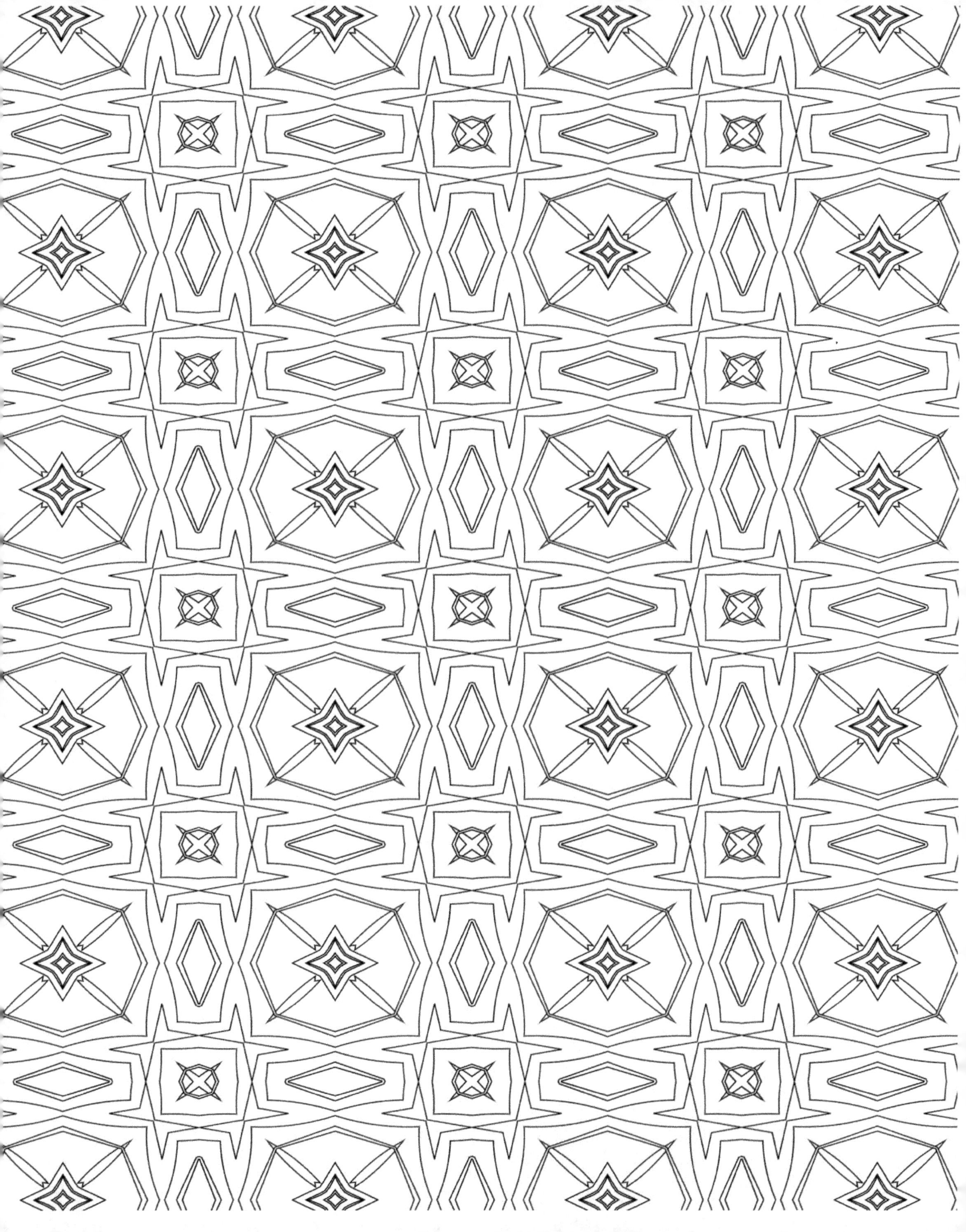

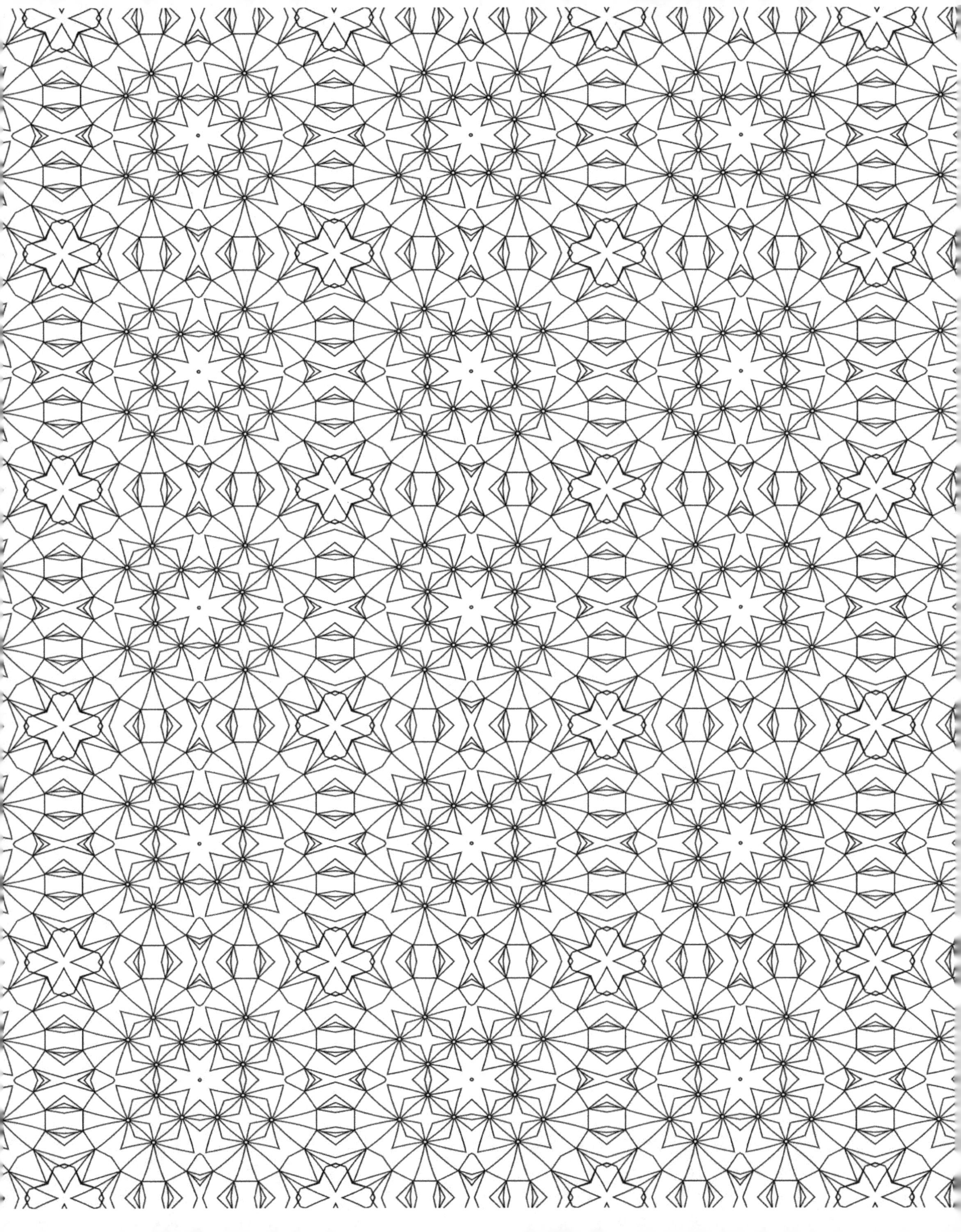

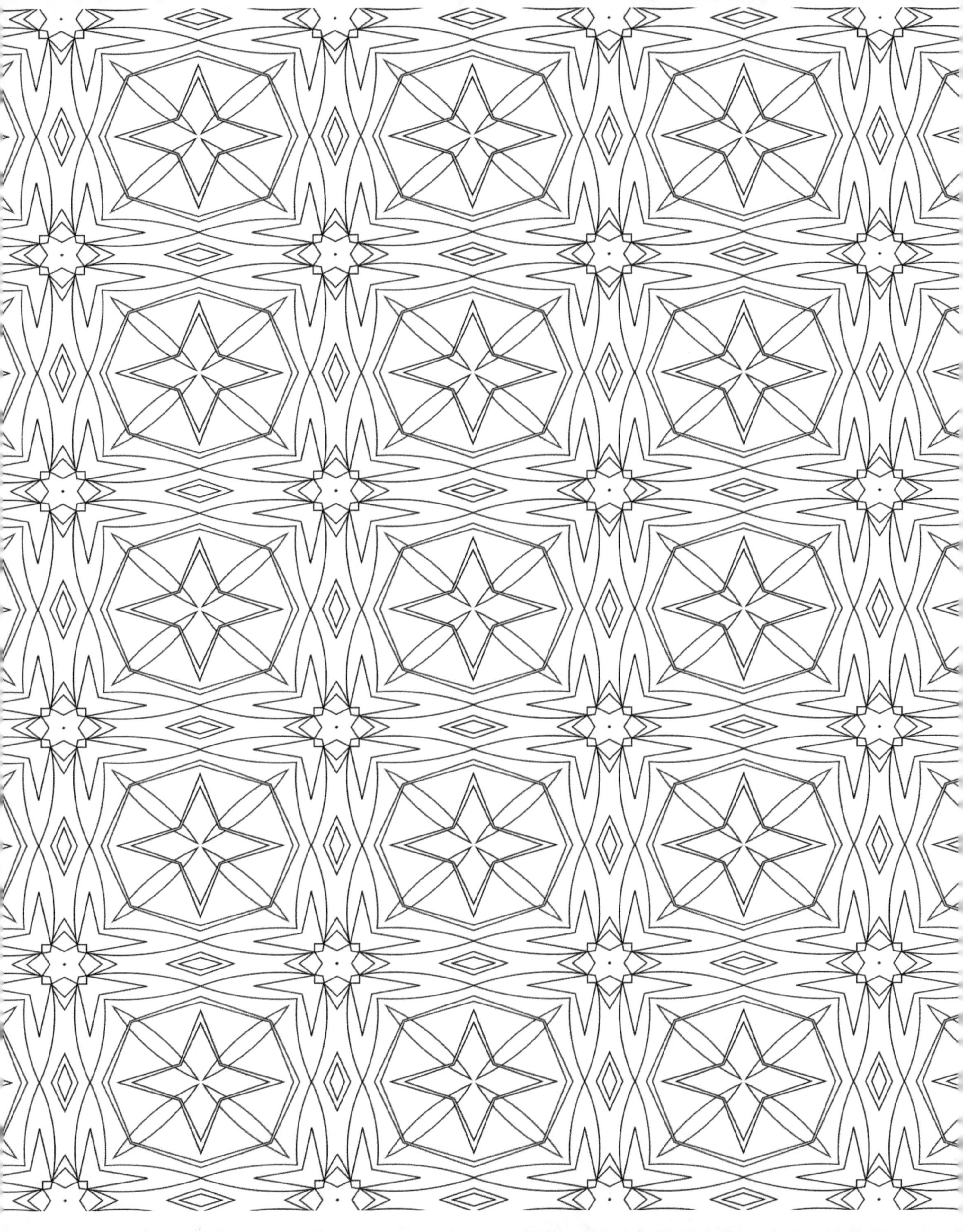

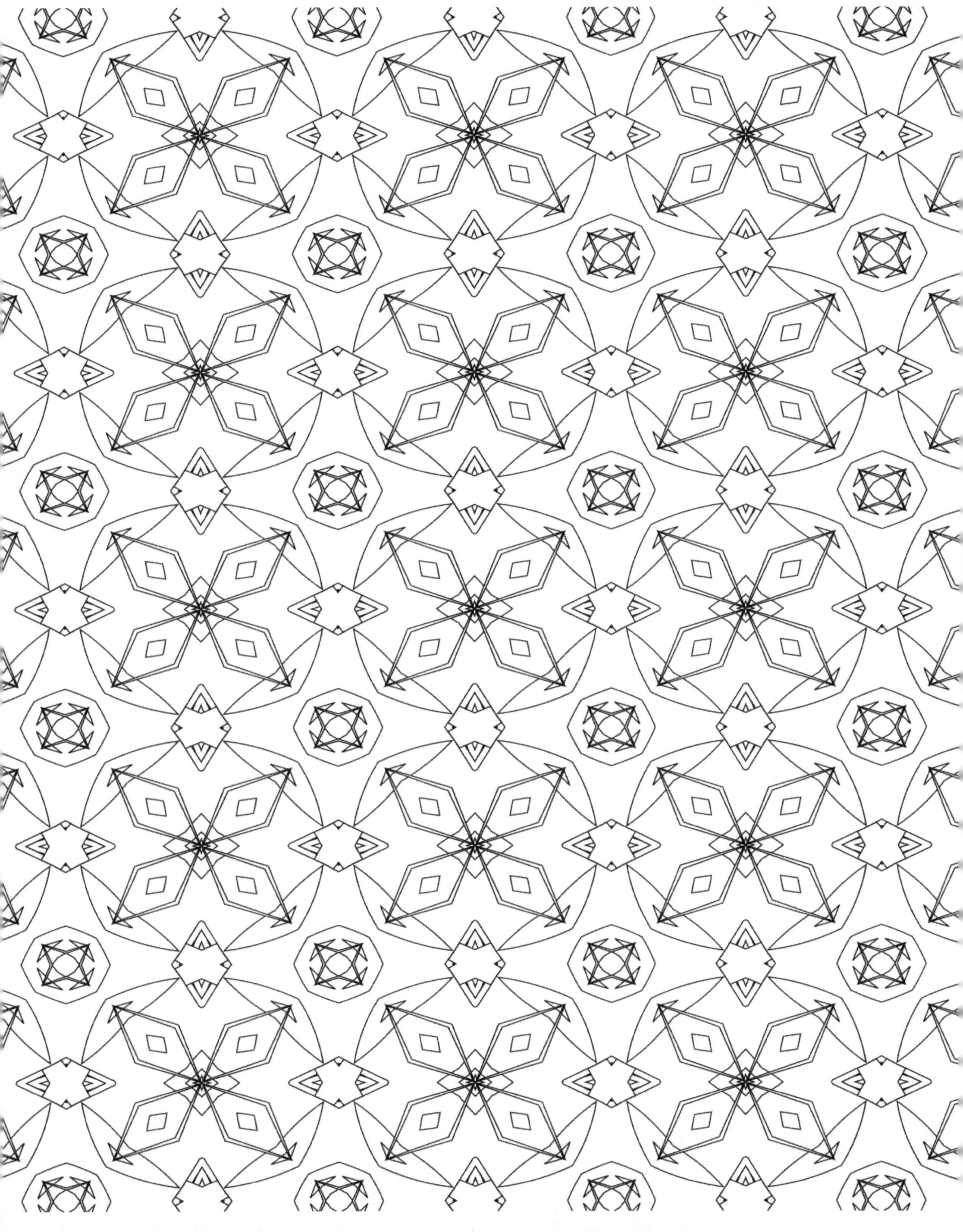

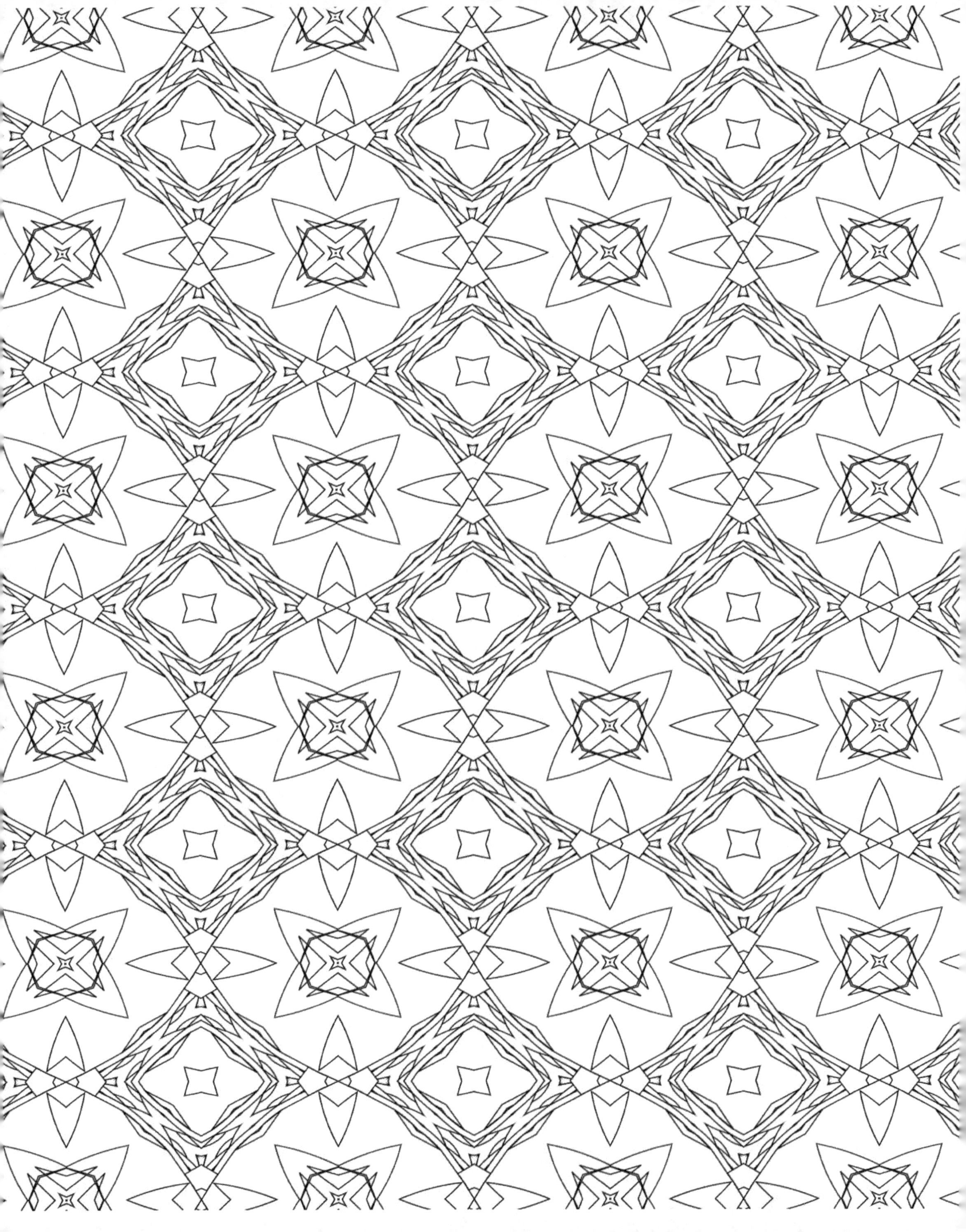

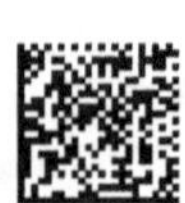
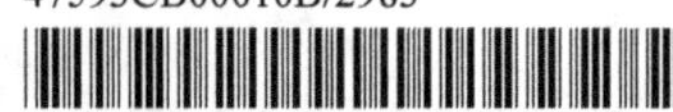